Christmas Around the World

Christmas in the

United States of America

By Christina Earley

Table of Contents

A Starfish Book

Teaching Tips for Caregivers:

As a caregiver, you can help your child succeed in school by giving them a strong foundation in language and literacy skills and a desire to learn to read.

This book helps children grow by letting them practice reading skills.

Reading for pleasure and interest will help your child to develop reading skills and will give your child the opportunity to practice these skills in meaningful ways.

- Encourage your child to read on her own at home
- Encourage your child to practice reading aloud
- Encourage activities that require reading
- Establish a reading time
- Talk with your child
- Give your child writing materials

Teaching Tips for Teachers:

Research shows that one of the best ways for students to learn a new topic is to read about it.

Before Reading

- Read the "Words to Know" and discuss the meaning of each word.
- Read the back cover to see what the book is about.

During Reading

- When a student gets to a word that is unknown, ask them to look at the rest of the sentence to find clues to help with the meaning of the unknown word.
- Ask the student to write down any pages of the book that were confusing to them.

After Reading

- Discuss the main idea of the book.
- Ask students to give one detail that they learned in the book by showing a text dependent answer from the book.

Christmas in the United States

MERRY CHRISTMAS

Christmas is celebrated by many people in the United States.

Lights are popular on houses and in city streets.

Some places have big **decorations**.

Fun Fact:
Some people make their lights dance to music.

Families have real or fake Christmas trees.

Everyone helps decorate with special **ornaments**.

The ***Nutcracker*** is a ballet that people enjoy watching.

It is about a girl who goes to a magical land with a prince.

Families bake different kinds of cookies.

They give them as presents to people in the community.

Nativities are set up in some homes. They show the story of Christmas.

Fun Fact:
Churches have live nativities with real people and animals.

BRISTOL CATHEDRAL CHOIR
BRISTOL CATHEDRAL CHOIR

Some families go to church on Christmas Eve.

They sing **carols**.

They watch the Christmas story acted out by children and adults.

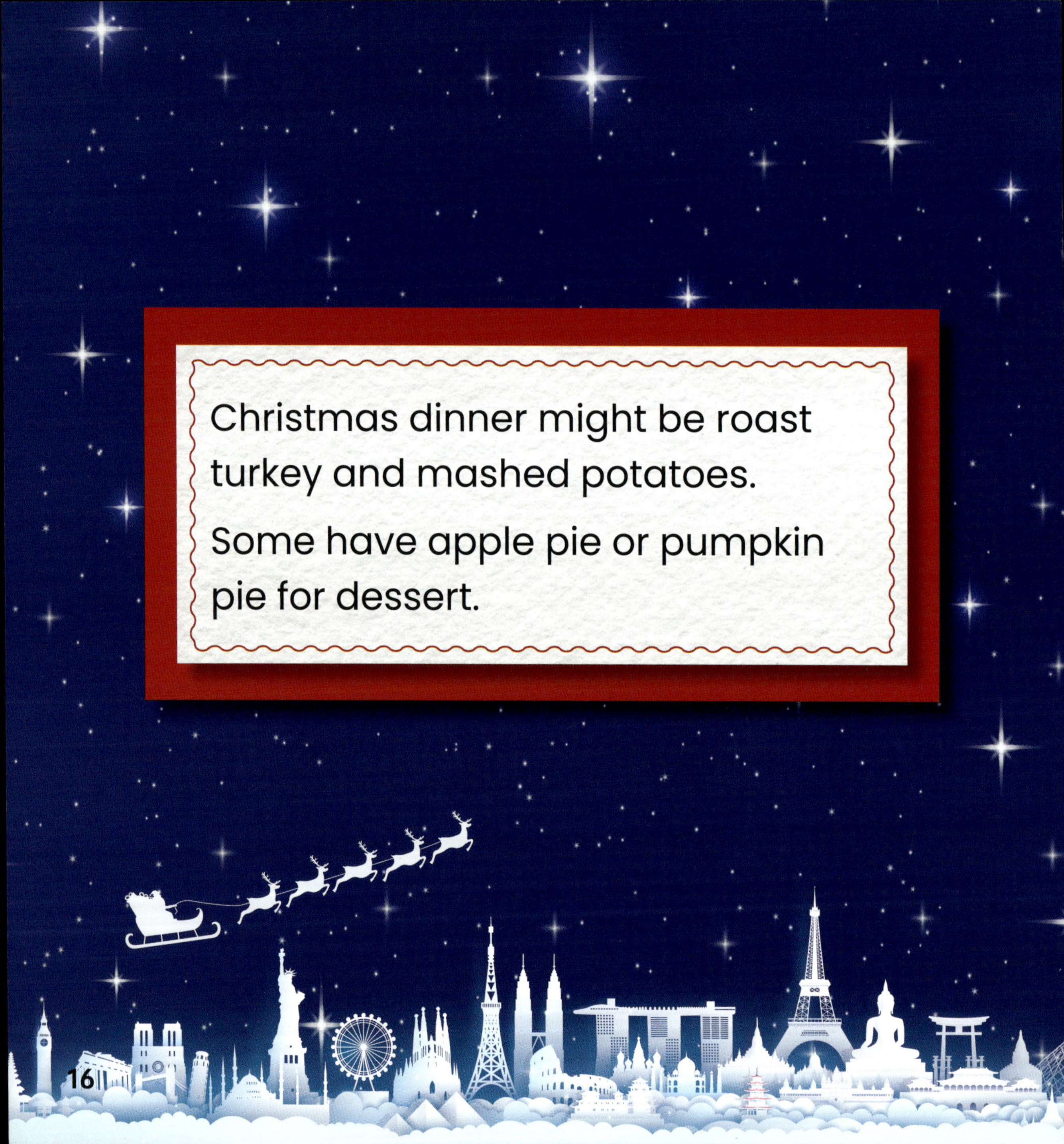

Christmas dinner might be roast turkey and mashed potatoes.

Some have apple pie or pumpkin pie for dessert.

Fun Fact:
People also cook traditional foods from other countries.

Dear Santa,
I have been good
this year. This
Christmas I
would like a
train set, a video
game, a warm
coat and hat.
I will leave you
cookies and
milk and some
carrots for
the reindeer
Love

Santa Claus brings presents on Christmas Eve.

He comes through the **chimney**.

Children open presents on Christmas Day.

Craft: Cinnamon Applesauce Ornaments

Materials

- 3 cups plain applesauce
- 3 cups ground cinnamon
- rolling pin
- cookie cutters
- toothpick
- ribbon (optional)

Steps

1. Mix the applesauce and cinnamon in a large bowl until a thick dough is formed.
2. Roll the dough onto a flat surface.
3. Cut out shapes using the cookie cutters. Use the toothpick to create a hole at the top.
4. Place on a cookie sheet and let dry for 3 to 4 days.
5. Thread ribbon through the hole. Tie the ends together to make a loop for hanging.

Recipe: Peanut Butter Blossoms

Ingredients

- 1 stick (½ cup) unsalted butter at room temperature
- ½ cup smooth peanut butter
- ½ cup white sugar, plus more for rolling
- ½ cup packed brown sugar
- 1 large egg
- 1½ cups all-purpose flour
- 1 teaspoon baking powder
- ½ teaspoon salt
- 24 chocolate kiss candies, unwrapped

Steps

1. Preheat the oven to 350° F (177° C).
2. In a medium bowl, mix the softened butter, peanut butter, white sugar, and brown sugar with a wooden spoon or electric mixer until smooth.
3. Add the egg and mix until combined.
4. In a separate medium bowl, combine the flour, baking powder, and salt.
5. Slowly add the dry ingredients to the wet ingredients until a thick dough forms.
6. Pour a few tablespoons of white sugar in a small bowl.
7. Scoop about 1½ tablespoons of dough. Roll into a ball using your hands. Roll in the sugar to coat.
8. Place the balls 2 to 3 inches (5 to 8 centimeters) apart on a baking sheet lined with parchment paper or a silicone mat.
9. Bake for 12 minutes or until domed on the top and golden brown.
10. Remove from oven and immediately press a chocolate kiss in the center of each cookie.
11. Allow cookies to cool for 5 minutes before removing from baking sheet.

Words to Know

carols (KAR-uhlz): traditional, joyful songs, especially those sung at Christmas

chimney (CHIM-nee): the upright part of a fireplace that guides smoke out through the roof

decorations (dek-uh-RAY-shuhnz): items people add to buildings or trees to make them festive

nativities (nuh-TIV-i-tees): stable scenes that show baby Jesus, Mary, Joseph, animals, shepherds, and angels

nutcracker (NUHT-krak-ur): a tool used to crack nuts; sometimes shaped like a toy soldier

ornaments (OR-nuh-muhnts): small decorations

Index

Comprehension Questions

1. *The Nutcracker* is a
   a. dessert.
   b. ballet.
   c. type of music.

2. A popular Christmas decoration for houses is
   a. lights.
   b. cards.
   c. balloons.

3. A traditional Christmas dinner is roast turkey and
   a. candy.
   b. fruit.
   c. mashed potatoes.

4. True or false: Santa Claus brings presents on Christmas Day.

5. True or false: Families decorate Christmas trees with special ornaments.

Answers
1. b 2. a 3. c 4. False 5. True

About the Author

Christina Earley lives in South Florida with her with husband, son, and dog named Bailey. Her favorite holiday is Christmas because it is a magical time of year. She collects ornaments that remind her of special places and events. She and her family have lots of fun baking cookies and eating candy canes while looking at Christmas lights.

Written by: Christina Earley
Design by: Jen Bowers
Editor: Kim Thompson

Library of Congress PCN Data
Christmas in the United States of America / Earley
Christmas Around the World
ISBN 978-1-63897-444-4 (hard cover)
ISBN 978-1-63897-559-5 (paperback)
ISBN 978-1-63897-674-5 (EPUB)
ISBN 978-1-63897-789-6 (eBook)
Library of Congress Control Number: 2022930315

Printed in the United States of America.

Photographs: Cover ©2020 Belikova Oksana/Shutterstock, pine ©Pasko Maksim/Shutterstock,world skyline©Painterstock/Shutterstock, background©ghenadie/Shutterstock, earth ©leonello/iStock; p.1 ©Mariana Mast/Shutterstock; p.3 ©2013 Veronica Louro/Shutterstock, ©deepstock/Shutterstock; p.5 ©2012 Fotomicar/Shutterstock, ornament©ekler/Shutterstock; p.7 ©2020 Drazen Zigic/Shutterstock; p.8 ©2014 Igor Bulgarin/Shutterstock; p.10 ©2020 Zerbor/Shutterstock; p.11 ©2017 Evgeny Atamanenko/Shutterstock; p.13 ©2013 PixelDarkroom/Shutterstock; p.14 ©2014 1000 Words/Shutterstock; p.17 ©2019 Alexander Raths/Shutterstock; p.18 ©2017 Gene Bleile/Shutterstock; p.19 ©2016 fotohunter/Shutterstock; p.20 ©2018 AWhitmorePhotography/Shutterstock; p.21 ©2015 Vezzani Photography/Shutterstock

Seahorse Publishing Company
www.seahorsepub.com

Published in the United States
Seahorse Publishing
PO Box 771325
Coral Springs, FL 33077